Living Religions

Buddhism

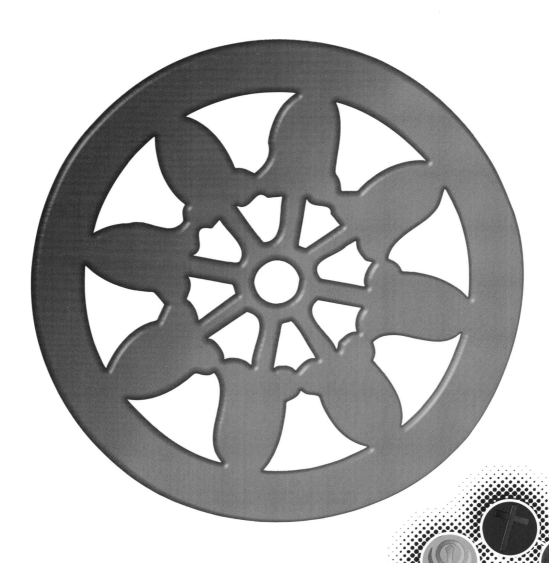

Cavan Wood

Raintree, 100 N. LaSalle St., Suite 1200, Chicago, IL 60602

Library of Congress Cataloging-in-Publication Data:

Wood, Cavan.
 Buddhism / Cavan Wood.
   v. cm. -- (Living religions)
Includes bibliographical references and index.
Contents: The birth of the Buddha -- The discontented prince -- The enlightenment of the Buddha -- The death of the Buddha -- Buddhist teaching on suffering -- Five moral precepts -- Nirvana, Karma, and Rebirth -- The Three Refuges -- Types of Buddhism -- Buddhist symbols -- The Bodhisattvas -- Buddhist devotion -- Meditation -- Buddhist holy places -- Buddhist scriptures -- The Festival of Wesak -- Other Buddhist festivals -- Buddhist pilgrimage -- Living in a monastery -- Being in a community -- Birth -- Marriage -- Death -- The environment -- Wealth and poverty -- Racism -- Key figures 1 -- Key figures 2.
 ISBN 0-7398-6382-7 (Library Binding-Hardcover)
 1. Buddhism--Juvenile literature. [1. Buddhism.] I. Title. II. Series.
 BQ4032 .W63 2003
 294.3--dc21
                              2002151939

Printed and bound in China.

07 06 05 04 03
10 9 8 7 6 5 4 3 2 1

Acknowledgments
The publishers would like to thank the following for permission to use photographs:

AKG London/Gilles Mermet, p. 7; Andes Press Agency/
C & D Hill, pp. 6 and 37 (bottom); Andes Press Agency/Carlos Reyes Manzo, pp. 16, 18, 19, 27 (top), 30, 47 and 57; Robin Bath, pp. 3, 8, 23 (top), 24, 25, 27 (bottom), 31 (middle and right), 38 and 58; Camerapress/Benoit Gysembergh, p. 59; Christine Osborne Pictures, pp. 10, 29, 34, 37 (top), 46, 48 (bottom), 50 and 52; Christine Osborne Pictures/Nick Dawson, p. 39; Christine Osborne/P Kapoor, p. 23 (bottom); Christine Osborne Pictures/S A Molton, p. 31 (left); Circa Photo Library/William Holtby, pp. 26, 36 and 40; Hutchison Library/Jon Burbank, p. 4 (bottom); Hutchison Library/Jeremy Horner, p. 48 (top); Karuna Trust, p. 53; Ann & Bury Peerless, p. 4 (top); Angela Walker, p. 41.

Contents

Introduction

In this section you will

- learn about the Buddhist religion and its place in a multicultural society;
- read about how Buddhism has influenced Western culture.

A religion without God?

You might think that in order for something to be a religion, you have to believe in God. While **Buddhism** is a religion, Buddhists do not have to believe in a god. Still, various forms of Buddhism believe in various gods, such as some Hindu gods that were revered when Buddhism began.

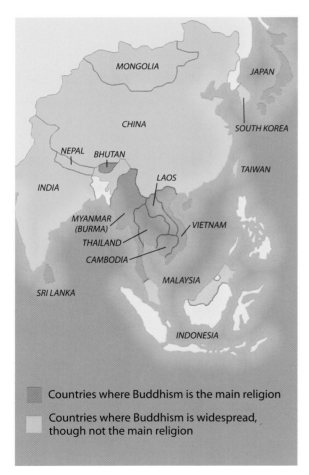

Countries where Buddhism is the main religion

Countries where Buddhism is widespread, though not the main religion

Countries where Buddhism is widespread today

Buddhism does have ideas about life and death, holy books, festivals, religious leaders, prayer, meditation, and special ceremonies to mark events such as birth, marriage, and death.

Buddhism began with the birth of **Siddhartha Gautama** in what is now Nepal around 563 B.C.E. About thirty-five years later, he became known as the **Buddha** and traveled through India until his death in 483 B.C.E.

The movement he started soon spread across the neighboring countries of Sri Lanka, Tibet, and Nepal. People in other Asian countries such as Japan, China, and Korea also converted to Buddhism.

As you can see from the map, Buddhism isn't limited to Asia. When the British Empire had control of India, many people traveled to the region and learned about the traditions there. Travelers to Japan and China also returned to Great Britain to tell about the religion of the Buddha.

In the early years of the twentieth century, The Buddhist Society was founded in London to explain and promote Buddhism in Britain. One member was Christmas Humphreys, who later became a very famous trial lawyer and a judge.

In the 1960s, Buddhism became more popular in the West. Many young people thought that Buddhist pacifist (anti-war) principles, vegetarianism, and stress on finding the truth for oneself rather than looking for the solutions from a god, fitted with their beliefs. Another important Buddhist belief is that of rebirth, the belief that human beings and all other life-forms go through many lifetimes until they reach the state of **nirvana,** the end of suffering and the release from the wheel of rebirth.

Musicians such as The Beatles have quoted from Buddhist books such as the Tibetan *Book of the Dead*. Artists have found inspiration from the **mandalas** and other Buddhist pictures.

An example of Buddhist art

Buddhism's teachings about rebirth, harmlessness (often including vegetarianism), nonviolence, and the use of meditation to find a way to truth have become popular. To many people, they seem to be a better alternative to what many were brought up to believe.

Many other young people found out about Buddhism when they were serving in Vietnam. The film director Oliver Stone became a Buddhist while serving there.

Buddhism has also become popular with many other people. They include the rock singers Tina Turner and musician Suzanne Vega and movie stars Richard Gere and Keanu Reeves. Movies such as *Kundun*, *Little Buddha,* and *Seven Years in Tibet* have shown that the interest in Buddhism continues to grow.

The Dalai Lama, the spiritual head of Tibet, is a well-known Buddhist leader. He was forced into exile in India following the Chinese invasion of Tibet in the 1950s.

In Burma the political leader and Buddhist, Aung San Suu Kyi, has become an internationally known figure for standing up against a military government that seized power when her party had won a majority in an election.

Facts about Buddhism

Buddhism is one of the major world religions. In countries all over the world, it has influenced many areas of life including the arts and gardening and physical activities such as the martial arts. Here are some interesting facts about Buddhism.

- Although Buddhism began in India, India now has one of the lowest numbers of practicing Buddhists in Asia.

- The exact number of Buddhists in the world is not known. Estimates range from 230 million to 500 million Buddhists worldwide.

- There are a number of different traditions in Buddhism, including Theravada Buddhism, **Mahayana** Buddhism (e.g., Zen Buddhism), and Vajrayana Buddhism (e.g., Tibetan Buddhism).

- Many gardening ideas come from the Zen Buddhist tradition, such as moss gardens and the use of sand, rocks, trees, ponds, and streams.

- The martial arts kendo, kung-fu, judo, and karate all began as forms of physical training by Buddhist monks, as did the relaxing art of t'ai-chi.

The Birth of the Buddha

In this section you will
- learn about the birth stories told about the Buddha and their symbolic meanings;
- read about India at the time of the Buddha's birth.

Queen Mayadevi's dream

Queen Mayadevi's dream

Some Buddhists believe that the Buddha existed in a heavenly realm before he came to earth. They believe he also had lived through several thousand other lifetimes—both animal and human—before he was born.

In the country of the Sakyas (a tribe that lived in areas that we call India and Nepal today) there lived a King named Suddhodana who was married to Queen Mayadevi. The Queen was very beautiful, fearless, and good. She told her husband of her great feelings of joy and peace one evening..

The Queen returned to her room and fell asleep. As she slept that night, she had a dream of a six-tusked white elephant, who had a head the color of rubies. This was a sign that Buddha himself had left heaven and was entering the world through her.

Explaining the dream

In the morning, the Queen told the King about her dream. The King decided to summon eight holy men to explain the dream.

They told him that the dream was a good sign. It meant that the Queen was pregnant and the baby would either be a great emperor or a great holy man.

Lumbini Grove today

The birth of the Buddha

The Queen and the King went to the woods of **Lumbini Grove** at the time the birth was expected. The Queen stepped from her chariot, followed by dancers and musicians.

She strolled until she was beneath the shade of a sala tree. As the tradition tells it, the tree bent down and the Queen took hold of a bending branch. As she looked into the sky, she saw the lucky stars of Pushya shining very brightly, a sign that great things were to happen.

It is said that as she stood there, the baby Buddha was born from her right side. Without any help, the child walked seven steps to the North, then the South, then the East, and then the West. At every step, a **lotus flower** sprang from the ground. His limbs shone as bright as gold. He seemed to beam light to all those around him. The child spoke: "No further births will I have to suffer, for this will be my last body. Now shall I destroy and pluck out the roots of the sorrow that is caused by the wheel of birth, life, and death."

When the King was told of the child's birth, he thought long and hard about what the boy should be called. He said, "I shall call him Siddhartha, meaning 'Perfect Fulfillment' because on the day of his birth all things were done to perfection."

Seven days after his birth, Queen Mayadevi died. Eventually, the King married Mayadevi's sister, Mahaprajapati, who cared for Siddhartha as if she were his birth mother.

A wise man called Asita came to see the baby and found 32 marks on the child that showed he would lead people to great truth. Asita began to weep, for he realized that he would not live long enough to see the child become the man who would teach people so many truths.

The King grew afraid of the talk of priests and wise men and decided to bring the boy up in such a way that he would not leave the palace for the wandering, religious life of a monk.

Background to the Buddha

India at the time of the birth of Siddhartha Gautama was a place where things were rapidly changing. It was a place where there was a great deal of intellectual and spiritual activity. People were growing increasingly unhappy with the ways they had been taught to see the world. They were beginning to travel more and to experience different ways of living. They were also impatient with a lot of what the religion of the day—Vedic Brahmanism, the forerunner of Hinduism—had to say.

As people began to move away from villages into large settlements such as towns and cities, they began to ask questions about why the world was in the state it was. They were becoming more questioning of their religious and political leaders.

Siddhartha Gautama came from the Sakya tribe, people who lived near the Ganges River basin. This was a tribe of warriors and noblemen. They felt that they were a lot better than the rest of the people in the area. Yet, even among these wealthy and powerful people, many were giving up their homes to follow wandering religious teachers. They wanted, more than anything, to find the meaning of their lives. The Buddha's teaching, following Siddhartha's enlightenment, offered an attractive alternative way to look at life.

The Discontented Prince

In this section you will
- learn how Prince Siddhartha became discontented with the life he was living, and the importance he came to attach to a search for meaning and truth;
- read about the Shramana movement in India.

Chained to unhappiness

According to Buddhist tradition, Prince Siddhartha grew up in a loving, happy environment. His father gave him his own palace, with all the servants he could ever want. He had all his needs attended to.

When he was a young man, he once protected a swan from an arrow shot from a bow by one of his friends. It is a story still told today not only to show how much he cared for the bird, but also as a way of saying that he knew what unhappiness meant.

Yet his father the King went to great lengths to keep his son from knowing about pain. Perhaps the King still felt the pain of having lost his wife so soon after the birth of his son. Whatever the cause, the King made sure that any servants who were ill or old or who died were removed so that Siddhartha would not see them.

The young Prince Siddhartha

The king feared that if Siddhartha saw these people, he might well ask questions that would lead him to the religious life that the King did not wish for his son.

So that was how Siddhartha lived. He was banned from going into the city, for fear that he would see the truth of life.

Siddhartha fell in love with the beautiful princess **Yashodhara.** All seemed perfect, especially when their first son was born. But Prince Siddhartha called him "**Rahula,**" which means "chain," a sign that he was very unhappy.

Visits to the city

One day, as the story goes, Siddhartha was talking to **Channa,** the man who drove the King's chariot. He asked Channa to take him into the city. Channa refused, but Siddhartha insisted, and eventually the chariot driver took him there.

On his first visit, Siddhartha saw an old man, leaning almost bent double on a stick. He asked what was wrong with him.

"He is old," said Channa. "One day, we shall all be like him, both princes and ordinary people."

On a second visit to the city, Siddhartha saw a sick man lying at the side of the road. Channa told him that illness happened to all, a reality that none could escape from.

Siddhartha was confused. Why had his father hidden these truths of existence from him? On a third visit, he saw the body of a dead man, lying and decaying at the side of the road. Channa told him that all people die.

Siddhartha returned to the palace, confused and wanting answers. On a fourth journey to the city, Siddhartha saw a bald man, carrying a bowl and dressed only in a simple robe. He asked Channa who this man was. Channa told him that this was a holy man, an **ascetic,** who had given up everything for the cause of truth.

Siddhartha cuts off his hair before his enlightenment.

Siddhartha decided that he must leave the palace in order to get to the truth. Early one morning, when everyone in the palace had fallen into a deep sleep, Siddhartha awoke and woke Channa, whom he ordered to take him to the forest where the holy men lived.

As he dismounted from the chariot at the edge of the wood, Siddhartha gave his princely cloak to Channa. Taking a knife, he cut off his ponytail. Now he would begin his search for truth with the holy men.

The Buddha and the Shramanas

When he became the Buddha, Siddhartha was often critical of the Shramana movement. However, over time he did come to share many of their central beliefs.

The word Shramana later came to mean a person who gave up the things of the world in order to practice Buddhism.

The Shramana movement

Many people at the time of the Buddha were trying to find a better way to live, and there was a lot of discussion about how to improve the religion of the area, which had a system of social classes.

When Siddhartha left the palace, a new religious movement had begun to be established in India. It was called the Shramana movement. The Shramanas believed that renunciation was the path to enlightenment, or liberation. They were asking questions about beliefs such as reincarnation, the soul, and whether practicing asceticism would 14lead to liberation.

The Jain religion of India is an example of this movement that still survives today.

The Enlightenment of the Buddha

In this section you will

● understand the importance of the enlightenment of the Buddha to Buddhists;

● read about how the Buddha reached enlightenment.

A flash of inspiration

The story goes that when the scientist Isaac Newton sat under an apple tree, an apple fell off. As he watched it, he realized that a force we call gravity was at work.

Alexander Fleming noticed that some mold on bread killed bacteria and, as a result of his work, we now have penicillin. Scientists can often see things that no one else has ever noticed.

The enlightened Buddha

Religious people have often regarded sudden flashes of inspiration as important, though they often say you may need to wait years to receive them.

Siddhartha leaves the holy men

After he left the palace, Siddhartha joined a group of holy men who practiced **asceticism**. This is the belief that denying your body things, you can overcome desires and free yourself from suffering. Siddhartha slept on thorns, ate mud, and at one point tried to live on no more than one grain of rice a day.

One day, as he was meditating, he heard a passing musician tell a pupil, "If the strings are too tight, they will break and not play. If they are too slack, they also will not play."

Siddhartha realized that he would not find the truth either living the life of pleasure that he had had as a prince or by denying himself as he had been doing with the holy men. The truth would lie between the two opposites, what he later called the **Middle Way.**

Siddhartha went to the river and there a local girl gave him a drink. He accepted her offer of food. The holy men were appalled and would not listen to him, seeing him as a traitor.

Siddhartha becomes the Buddha

As the story continues, Siddhartha left the holy men and went to a place called **Bodh Gaya.** He decided to sit under a bodhi tree, waiting there until he had reached full understanding of the big questions in life.

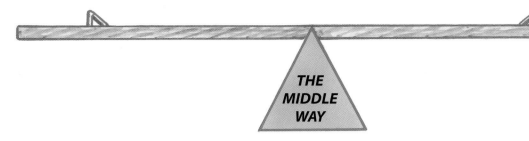

The Middle Way lies between self-denial and self-indulgence.

According to Buddhists, a devil figure called **Mara** tried to keep Siddhartha from the truth. First Mara sent his daughters to try to keep Siddhartha from his quest. These daughters were human incarnations of lust, ignorance, and greed. When Siddhartha ignored them, Mara gave him the illusion first that he was in the middle of a great storm and then that he was being attacked by a great army. But still Siddhartha continued to meditate.

Finally, Mara appeared as the exact image of Siddhartha. But Siddhartha saw through the deception and he resisted these attacks.

During the night that followed, Siddhartha came to understand the other lives he had had. He also realized the nature of suffering and that freedom from suffering could be found. The truth of suffering he identified in what he called the **Four Noble Truths** and the **Eightfold Path,** which he saw as a path to a way that gives people freedom or liberation.

He was no longer Siddhartha but the Buddha. "Buddha" means "the enlightened or awoken one." Siddhartha had "awakened" to what life was really about.

After enlightenment

After the Buddha was enlightened, it enabled him to see the reality of the way things were in the world. There are many different accounts of what the Buddha went on to do, and the order of the stories differ. One tradition suggests that he may have seen a god called Brahma Sahampati, who told him that he had, indeed, found the truth. The Buddha at this point was not sure whether people were ready to hear his teaching, but the story says that Brahma Sahampati asked him to start teaching people.

The Buddha's followers did not believe him to be a god. Although one of the "six realms of rebirth" is that of the devas, or gods, the devas are not considered ultimate beings but are still on the wheel of rebirth just as the rest of us.

The Death of the Buddha

The story of Kisagami

"We die all the time, from moment to moment, and what is really there is a perpetual succession of extremely shortlived events."

Edward Conze

The Buddha as a teacher

For 45 years, the Buddha traveled the length of India teaching his ideas. He gathered a group of disciples, who eventually included the holy men who had once rejected him, his son Rahula, and one of his most important disciples, **Ananda.**

Over seven years, every cell in your body dies and is replaced by another. There is a very real sense in which we are dying all the time .

One day, an unhappy woman named **Kisagotami** came to the Buddha. Her child had recently died and, in her shock, she carried him around. She came to the Buddha, asking that he perform a miracle and cure the child.

ဘုရားသည် တရာကာသိ ပြည် အနီးရှိ မိဂဒါဝန် တော်၌ ကောဏ္ဍည-ဝပ္ပ-ဘဒ္ဒိယ-မဟာနာမ-အဿဇိ ဟူသော ပဥ္စဝဂ္ဂီ ငါးဦးတို့
ရှင်ကောဏ္ဍညသည် ဦးစွာသောတပန်အဖြစ်သို့ရောက်ပြီး အနတ္တလက္ခဏာသုတ်ကို ဆက်လက်၍ဟောတော်မူရာ ပဥ္စဝဂ္ဂ
ဖြစ်လာကြသဖြင့် ဘုရားရှင်၏သာသနာတွင်ပထမဦးဆုံးသော သံဃာတော်များ ဖြစ်ကြလေသည်။

ဘိ:ဦး:ဥတ္တမသာရ-မြို့နယ် သံဃာနာယကအဖွဲ့အမှူးဆောင်-ကောဓမယ်ကိုက်ကောဂင်-ကော

The Buddha and his disciples

The Buddha realized that she had not really accepted the death of the child and so he set her a task to make her come to terms with the reality.

"Go and collect mustard seeds from every house where death has not visited and then return with them and I will help you."

Kisagotami traveled and knocked on every door she could find. But the answer was always the same—many people had died over the years in each of the houses she visited. She returned to the Buddha and quietly lay the body of her child at his feet.

She looked at him with tears in her eyes and said, "Now I realize that I am not alone in my grief and that all will be touched by death."

The Buddha told her that she must now bury her child. From that day on, Kisagotami was a Buddhist.

The death of the Buddha

The Buddha was 80 years old when the time came for him to die. According to Buddhist belief, he hinted to his assistant Ananda that he would soon die but Ananda did not understand.

The Buddha had his disciples come to stay at **Kushinagara,** where tradition says he entered into *parinirvana* at the time of his death. On a visit to a follower named **Chunda,** Buddha ate something that gave him food poisoning (probably a mushroom).

The funeral pyre was not lit until the Malian monks were able to reach the scene. The passing of the Buddha was greeted with music, dancing, and joy—he had achieved his goal and had helped so many other people to understand the truth. To be sad seemed wrong on this occasion. In his teaching, the Buddha had said, "Every moment we are born, decay, and die, but we continue and are reborn elsewhere."

After the funeral fire died down, the traditional stories tell us that there were 84,000 relics of the Buddha left. These have been preserved in Buddhist buildings across Asia. These buildings include a **stupa** in the city of Kandy in Sri Lanka. This is said to contain one of the Buddha's teeth (see pages 36–37).

Teachings about death

The Buddha taught a great deal about death during his lifetime. Some of his teaching was recorded in the part of the Buddhist scriptures known as the Dharmapada. Here are some examples of Buddhist beliefs about death.

"When a man considers this world as a bubble of froth, and as the illusion of an appearance, then the king of death has no power over him. This world is indeed darkness, and how few can see the light! Just as a few birds escape from the net, so few souls fly into the freedom of heaven."
Dharmapada 170, 174

"There is no suffering for him who has finished his journey and abandoned grief, who has freed himself on all sides and thrown off all fetters [chains]."
Dharmapada 90

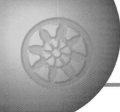

Buddhist Teaching on Suffering

In this section you will

● learn about the importance to Buddhists of the Four Noble Truths and the Eightfold Path;

● read about the qualities which the Buddha considered important.

The Buddha's teaching

The Buddha taught that there were Four Noble Truths.

1. Old age, sickness, and death will happen to us all—we all suffer.

2. Suffering comes from grasping (attachment).

3. If we give up attachment, suffering can end.

4. People should use their skills and follow the Eightfold Path.

The Buddha wanted people to realize the truths about life. He thought that the desires, the longings people have to own things, to have certain relationships or any other sorts of longings only lead to pain, because the things we long for cannot be permanent.

When the Buddha said that there was no such thing as a self, he was saying that humans are a continuous process of different parts and events that come together for a time. A Buddhist named **Nagasena** once wrote that the self was a little like a chariot. A chariot is made up of parts such as a wheel or an axle, so there really is no such thing as a chariot, but a collection of parts. What we call a self is made up of things such as physical form, feelings, perceptions, and thoughts, all of which are impermanent and always changing. What we need, he said, is to realize that we are believing an illusion if we think we are always going to remain the same.

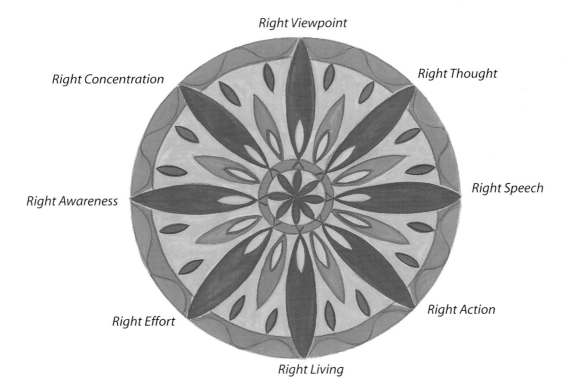

The Eightfold Path

By following the Eightfold Path, Buddhists believe they can find a way to end suffering and see beyond the illusion.

The Eightfold Path is not eight individual steps, but rather a way that needs to be taken as a whole. The eight steps are:

1 Right Understanding: understanding the truths that the Buddha has given.

2 Right Intention: following the path for the right reasons.

3 Right Speech: speaking in a way that does not dwell on the self. Speaking to others in a way that shows respect, is harmless, and avoids rudeness or dishonesty.

4 Right Action: living life in such a way as to follow the teachings of the Buddha by attempting to keep the **Five Moral Precepts.**

5 Right Livelihood: choosing a job that does not lead to arrogance or violence. Most Buddhists would avoid professions such as butchery or the armed forces because they would have to use violence in order to do their job.

6 Right Effort: **meditating** and making sure to do the right things in order to become indifferent to success.

7 Right Mindfulness: becoming aware through meditation of all that you do in thought, speech, and action.

8 Right Concentration: freeing yourself from worry, anxiety, and envy in order to think clearly.

Buddhists also believe they should develop four essential qualities: metta (loving kindness), karuna (compassion), mudita (sympathetic joy), and upekkah (serenity).

Four truths—four qualities

As well as accepting the Four Noble Truths, the Buddha wanted his followers to develop four qualities that would make them better people. These qualities are attitudes toward other people. They are:

● **Metta,** or loving kindness, which should make us gentler toward each other. Metta always seeks to put the other person first, and to care about others before ourselves.

● **Karuna,** or compassion, which enables us to feel the pain of others and to help relieve their pain.

● **Mudita,** finding joy in other people's happiness. We should try not to be discontented when others succeed and we do not. Mudita is the opposite of envy and jealousy.

● **Upekkha,** finding peace and balance in whatever happens to us. Upekkha is an ability to remain calm in any crisis.

Five Moral Precepts

In this section you will

● learn about the Five Moral Precepts taught by the Buddha;

● read about why many Buddhists are vegetarians and the Buddha's view on vegetarianism.

Avoid taking what is not given.

Good intentions

A promise is an important commitment. It is very important to always keep our promises, large or small. It seems that people who cannot keep their promises in small things will not be able to keep their word on big things. The Buddha called on his followers to follow five **intentions** to live a good life. These solemn promises are called the Five Moral Precepts.

Five intentions

The Buddha made suggestions based on his own experience and understanding rather than making rules that told his followers what to do.

His five suggestions were:

1 **To avoid taking life.** This intention was to extend to both animal and human life, so many Buddhists are vegetarians, and many are pacifists. Many Buddhists would say that this promise also means that they should try to be aware of the implications of abortion and euthanasia. There may be occasions where taking a life is unavoidable, but the intention not to cause harm is the main focus. Buddhists believe in **ahimsa,** which means avoidance of violence if at all possible.

2 **To avoid taking what is not given.** This is a promise not to steal. Some Buddhists say that this does not just refer to stealing possessions. It includes stealing someone else's ideas or reputation by claiming to have done something when you have not, perhaps taking credit for someone else's accomplishments.

3 **To avoid sexual misconduct.** Buddhists believe that they should live their lives in ways that do not hurt other people. Since sex is so important, they believe that it should take place in committed relationships.

Avoid lying and gossip.

4 **To avoid speaking falsely.** This is a promise not to lie or gossip or wound someone by words. Buddhists believe that people should always try to tell each other the truth but in a respectful way. People should always listen to others' points of view. This intention also encourages Buddhists not to speak too much or too loudly.

5 **To avoid drink and drugs that can cloud the mind.** Buddhists believe that it is **unskillful** to get drunk. Similarly, they are not against using drugs for medical reasons, but they do not feel that taking drugs to the point of "heedlessness" is helpful because they feel it is a way to avoid reality rather than face it.

The Buddha believed that if people kept these promises, they would be able to grow in wisdom and understanding of what is **skillful,** or right, and what is lacking in skill, or that which is likely to cause suffering. The Buddha also believed that if people followed these promises, they would develop **karuna,**, a compassionate love for all others.

Buddhism and vegetarianism

Many Buddhists are vegetarians as a result of teachings such as the first **Moral Precept,** which is to avoid taking life. As the Buddhist writer Sagaramati put it in *Golden Drum* magazine:

"If one is trying to practice the teaching of the Buddha by being kinder and more compassionate to all creatures, it is quite obvious that one relatively easy step is withdrawing from the meat of animal flesh. Surely in our age, no form of meat eating is entirely blameless."

There are also Buddhists who do eat meat, for example, Mahayana Buddhists in Japan and Tibet. Some Budhists eat meat because they get all their food from begging and must eat whatever is put in their bowls. Some believe the Buddha himself was not a vegetarian.

Nirvana, Karma, and Rebirth

In this section you will

● learn about nirvana, karma, and rebirth, which are very important ideas to Buddhists;

● read about what Buddhists do to reach the goal of nirvana.

The promise of a paradise

Human beings have often longed to find a place where they can live good lives and where all things will be easy. Humans have dreamed of finding a paradise where they will be able to live freely.

Buddhists believe that the ultimate goal is to reach **nirvana.** This is not a place, but a state of being that Buddhists believe they will reach when they have overcome the dream of having a self, are freed from suffering, and are no longer being reborn.

Rebirth

Buddhists believe that we are trapped on a **wheel of life.** They believe that we will be reborn many times due to the **karma** we develop through ignorance and attachment.

Buddhists believe that, unaware, we may be reborn as humans or animals. Sometimes a particular rebirth is for a reason, for example, to teach a particular quality. A very proud person might be reborn as an insect as a way of learning humility.

Buddhists believe that when you are reborn as a human being, you should not waste the opportunity this gives you, because it is only as a human being that you will be able to reach **enlightenment.** Only human beings have the mental capacity to reach enlightenment. The Buddha once said that the chances of being born a human being were the same as those

Liberation means freedom from suffering and the experience of true calm and peace.

of a blind turtle's being able in 100 years to swim through a ring in a vast ocean.

What goes around, comes around

There are consequences to every action. Perhaps you have said something unpleasant about someone else and they have found out, causing a bad feeling between both of you. Or perhaps you have tried to get out of doing your homework, only to be kept after school.

On the other hand, you might do something good for someone else and have the satisfaction of seeing them benefit from your actions.

Buddhists believe that the rebirths that we undergo are a result of the karma we have. Karma is the effect of our actions. Every action has a reaction. If people do good, then good will follow. If people choose to do evil, then evil will follow—or as you sow so you will reap. The results of karma can be experienced in the present lifetime, even day by day.

In Buddhism, karma can carry over from one lifetime to another and therefore Buddhists feel it is vital that people try to live the best life they can, since they will often have to make up for the bad karma of previous lifetimes. Karma will determine whether people reach enlightenment or have to live 1,000 lifetimes as a lesser animal in order to get to the truth.

Karma does not only work for individuals but can also have an effect on the whole nation or the whole planet. Buddhists talk about collective karma, when the consequences of actions taken by whole countries can often change things. For example, Buddhists would argue that the way rich nations treat the poorer nations of the world may well affect the karma of a whole country or a group such as the United Nations.

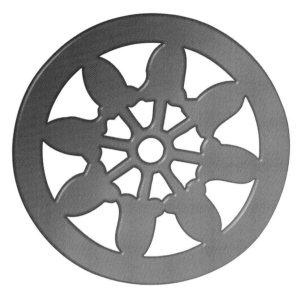

The wheel of life

Reaching nirvana

There are many different ways in which a Buddhist might make it easier to get to the ultimate goal of nirvana. The following are two ways:

- **Dana.** This is the idea that we should try to be generous. Some Buddhists, for example, give to charities that help people in developing nations.

- **Sila.** This is the idea that all moral actions should be skillful (appropriate), and that they should help make it possible for people everywhere to live free of the delusions and desires that Buddha warned against.

The Three Refuges

A person to follow

Different people can help us in different ways. A police officer might warn us if there are traffic problems ahead. A tour guide will help get us to the destination we want to visit on vacation. A team coach will give us advice and support in sports.

Buddhists believe in what they call the **Three Refuges** (sometimes also called the Three Jewels). These refuges are designed to help them, but Buddhists believe these supports exist within a person.

The first of the Three Refuges is remembered in the vow:

"I go to the Buddha for refuge."

The symbol for the Three Refuges

Buddhists feel that to be a Buddha is to be a being who is awake to the way the world is, who is wise and can see clearly. Buddhists believe that people can use their own experiences to see clearly and throw light on a situation. Experience can show clearer pathways if people reflect on the pathways they have already used and know. Insight is a person's own trusted gut feeling or inner voice of wisdom. Refuge can be found in the confidence that these feelings bring.

The Dharma

The second of the Three Refuges is expressed:

"I go to the Dharma for refuge."

The **Dharma** is the Buddhist word for the teaching of the Buddha, which can be found in scriptures such as the **Pali Canon.** The word "dharma" literally means "the Law" or "the Way," a truth that needs to be responded to and lived out in practice.

Buddhists may consult specially trained teachers of the scriptures, such as monks, to understand all the teachings of the Buddha. They may also use meditation to find the truth for themselves. Some Buddhists, such as those who follow Zen Buddhism, often have teachers who make wise statements and tell stories to help their students understand the Dharma.

Reading the Dharma

We all have a need to belong to a group.

The need to belong

Everyone needs a sense of belonging to feel secure. Families and friends can help us out and stick by us when we feel troubled or unloved.

The third of the Three Refuges is stated as:

"I go to the Sangha for refuge."

For some Buddhists, the word "**sangha**" means a community of Buddhists who live as monks and nuns. However, most Buddhists believe that the Sangha is the community of all who belong to a local **vihara** or temple, or, more broadly, the community of all Buddhists worldwide.

It is very important for Buddhists to belong to a Sangha because this enables them to take a fully active part in the festivals of their religion. It enables them to share their insights and understandings gained through meditation and prayer, as well as to share problems they face. The Sangha is a community of like-minded spiritual friends, supporting and encouraging each other in the development of their faith.

Stories about the Buddha

There are many stories about the Buddha that help to show the meaning of his teaching. One of these stories tells about the Buddha when he was still known as Prince Siddhartha. His father was taking part in a plowing festival. Siddhartha closed his eyes and began to feel that his mind was in a swirl but, as he began to take hold of his thoughts, he felt at peace. When the king and his friends returned, someone looked at Siddhartha and said, "He looks to have the calmness of a holy man."

The peace that Siddhartha experienced at that moment was the peace he would eventually find as the Buddha, and would share with his followers then and now through his Dharma.

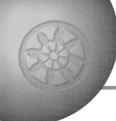

Types of Buddhism

In this section you will
● learn about the similarities and differences between the two main types of Buddhism;
● read about other types of Buddhism.

Witness to a crime

Imagine a crime has been committed. When it comes to trial, the witnesses may not agree about many of the details. They may disagree about the facts of what had happened, why things happened, in what order they occurred, and what they mean.

Yet in a court of law, it might still be possible to convict someone of a crime, even if all the witnesses do not agree on all the key parts. They may differ, but together they can give you enough detail to develop a picture of the truth.

The blind men and the elephant

A witness to a crime can be crucial to solving it.

Blind men and elephants

A famous Buddhist story tells of a king who asked a group of blind men to each feel a part of an elephant and describe what they thought an elephant was like. The one who held the trunk thought it was like a snake, the one who touched the leg thought it was like a tree trunk, and so on. They did not accurately define the truth by themselves, yet their poetic descriptions of the elephant each had a certain truth.

Many Buddhists would say that the different types of Buddhism can never by themselves get to the whole truth, but that together they are pointers in the general direction of the truth.

Theravada Buddhism

"**Theravada**" means "the teaching of the elders." Theravada Buddhism bases its teachings on the material in the Pali Canon (the original texts).

Theravada Buddhists believe that the Buddha was only a man, not superhuman.

Theravada Buddhists believe that the religious life is more easily available to those who live as monks and nuns who are supported in their practice by the **Sangha.** They stress that **merit** can be achieved by trying to follow the Six Perfections:

1. morality (**sila**)

2. generosity (**dana**)

3. patience (**kshanti**)

4. energy (**virya**)

5. concentration (**dhyana**)

6. wisdom (**prajna**)

Mahayana Buddhism

Mahayana Buddhism began in the first century B.C.E. One of its most well-known forms is Zen Buddhism.

Mahayana Buddhists believe that all people can become Buddhas. They still do believe that the Buddha was the most perfect example.

They talk of the Buddha as having three bodies:

1. transformation body—the body he had when he was alive;

2. enjoyment body—the body with which he can visit people in visions today;

3. dharma body—the "truth" body that is the teachings the Buddha or **Bodhisattvas** left behind for their followers.

Mahayana Buddhists also stress the importance of Bodhisattvas, "the Buddhas to be," who decide to stay back from nirvana and who continue to be reborn in this world or exist in another realm to help lead the rest of the faithful in finding the truth.

Vajrayana Buddhism

There are other kinds of Buddhism, too. A third type is Vajrayana, which includes Tibetan Buddhism.

Pure Land Buddhism

The most popular kind of Buddhism in Japan is known as Pure Land Buddhism. It teaches that faith in Amida Buddha, the Buddha of Infinite Light and Life, cuts the bonds to all negative things in our lives. Amida Buddha is said to have created a "Pure Land" where people go after death to reach nirvana and become Buddhas.

Nichiren Shoshu Buddhism

One type of Buddhism is called Nichiren Shoshu Buddhism. It was started in Japan in the 13th century by Nichiren Daishonin. Nichiren Daishonin was educated in a Buddhist temple where, when he was only 15 years old, he became a monk. Later he came to believe that what he taught was "true Buddhism." He believed that his form of Buddhism, which saw the Lotus Sutra as the highest teaching, completed what the Buddha had begun.

Nichiren Shoshu Buddhism was a very small movement until the 1960s, when Diasaku Ikeda became its new leader. Ikeda wrote more than 100 books on the movement's beliefs. Nichiren Shoshu Buddhism claims that if you chant for things you need, they will come to you.

Buddhist Symbols

In this section you will

- find out about some of the important symbols of the Buddhist tradition and their meaning;

- read about mudras, which are symbolic hand positions used by Buddhists.

Read the signs

Symbols can have a number of uses. They can warn us about something, such as a dangerous road ahead. They can give us instructions and they can give us information. In the religious world, signs and symbols can act in these ways, as well many others.

Meditating helps Buddhists gain peace.

The lotus flower

The lotus flower is an important symbol for Buddhism. It means "transformation," and is a symbol of purity and growth. The beautiful lotus flower can be found on the surface of a lake. Its roots are buried deep within the mud of the lake. The Buddha saw this as a symbol for human life—we may be stuck in the mud of human existence, but we can still come to an enlightenment in the midst of the murk.

One of the important Buddhist scriptures is called the **Lotus Sutra**. In meditation, some Buddhists sit in the lotus position, with each foot resting on the opposite thigh, to help them gain peace.

The wheel of life

The wheel of life is another important symbol. The eight spokes in the wheel stand for the Eightfold Path that the Buddha advised people to follow. It reminds Buddhists that they are all trapped on the cycle of birth-death-birth from which they can escape only when they stop being attached to being "someone living somewhere." By letting go and entering into the state of **nirvana,** Buddhists experience a boundless state of freedom and oneness with the universe.

In the center of the wheel of life are the cockerel, the snake, and the pig. They stand for the three poisons that can corrupt the mind—greed, hatred, and ignorance (or delusion). Over the top of the wheel is Yama, a demon who reminds us that this is a world of change and decay.

The six realms inside the wheel represent the six possible types of rebirth: hell beings, hungry ghosts, animals, human beings, titans, and gods. These six realms can also be understood as states of mind that we can experience every day, throughout the day.

Making a mandala with colored sand

Buddha rupas

There are many different images of the Buddha, which are called **rupas.** A sitting Buddha shows the importance of meditation. The Buddha in the lotus position shows him teaching the **Dharma.**

There are other images that remind Buddhists of their religion. For example, a riderless horse stands for the sacrifice the Buddha made when he left the palace to join the holy men.

Another way of showing beauty in a world of constant change and decay is by making **mandalas.** These are special patterns, sometimes made from colored sand to show that they can never remain permanent.

A sitting Buddha rupa

Mudras

In Buddhism, a number of hand positions are symbolic of ways of being. These different hand positions are known as **mudras.** They are often shown on rupas, or images of the Buddha, found in shrines.

A Buddhist may show an open hand as a way of showing an effort to become more generous. This position is called a dana-mudra, because dana is the word used in the language of the Buddhist scriptures to mean generosity. In the dhyana mudra, the hands are held flat in the lap with the palms facing upward. This mudra shows a state of contemplation.

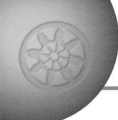

The Bodhisattvas

In this section you will

- learn about the importance to Mahayana Buddhists of the idea of the Bodhisattvas, the enlightened beings who try to help people to reach enlightenment;
- read about the Buddhist teaching of trikaya.

Avalokitesvara

Heroes or zeros

Many of us like stories about heroes and superheroes such as Superman or Batman. Perhaps we admire their bravery.

Or perhaps we admire a famous sports personality or pop star. We may try to read everything they say. We may try to live our lives in the way they live theirs. Sometimes they can be role models of how to live a good life or they can show us how to avoid a bad life. Choosing a good role-model is something we all need to do.

Enlightened beings

In Mahayana Buddhism, there is a group of beings called **Bodhisattvas.** They are "Buddhas to be," beings who have attained enlightenment but choose to stay back from **nirvana** so that they can lead others to enlightenment. Sometimes, these beings may return as human beings. For instance, Tibetan Buddhists think that the **Dalai Lama** is a Bodhisattva.

Bodhisattvas are also often symbols for a characteristic that the Buddha had or that the individual Buddhist should try to obtain. The most important of these characteristics are wisdom and compassion.

Avalokiteshvara

This Bodhisattva stands for perfect compassion. He is eager to help Buddhists find solutions to the problems they face in their daily lives as well as to help them reach the goals of enlightenment and nirvana.

Tara

Tara is a female Bodhisattva who is said to have been born from the teardrops shed by Avalokitesvara when he saw the suffering of human beings. She is said to be a compassionate Bodhisattva who comes to the aid of all who need her and call on her.

Tara

Maitreya

Maitreya

For many Buddhists, Maitreya is the most important of the Bodhisattvas. They believe that he will one day come to earth and bring in a golden age of wisdom and peace. His teachings will be so powerful and his leadership so wise that he will be known as a second Buddha. Although he currently lives in a heavenly realm, he appears to people who experience a heavenly state in order to reveal truths and lead them to enlightenment.

The three bodies

In Mahayana Buddhism in about 300 C.E., a teaching called "**trikaya**" began. This teaching said that Buddhas and Bodhisattvas had three different bodies. Just as water can exist in three different ways (liquid, steam, or ice), so the Buddhas and Bodhisattvas had different bodies representing different parts of their nature.

● The first body was the physical body— the body in which a Buddha or a Bodhisattva taught. This body was known as the nirmana-kaya.

● The second body was the enjoyment body—the body that could be seen by Buddhists in a vision or when they were in a state of meditation. This body was called the sambhoga-kaya.

● The third body was the truth body— the teachings, the acts, and the wisdom that transcend the physical body of the Buddha or Bodhisattva. It was known as the dharma-kaya.

Buddhist Devotion

Being a fan

To be a fan is to be a great admirer of something. If you follow a football team you may want to own a t-shirt or jacket with the team's logo. You may want to have a poster. You may also want to go to the games or at least watch them on television. If you are into music, you may want posters and CDs, and you may want to see the artist you like in concert.

People who are fans believe that they need to show the worth of what they think is important by doing things to show their devotion.

Showing respect to the Buddha

Paying respect at home

Buddhists often visit a **vihara** (temple) or monastery to help them in their spiritual life.

Many Buddhists also have a shrine in their home. This contains an image of the Buddha, called a rupa, as well as flowers, candles, incense, and pictures of Bodhisattvas.

They will recite the **Three Refuges** and the Five Moral Precepts at the shrine. They may meditate in front of it to help them to focus. They will often burn incense to show their devotion to the Buddha.

Prayer

Many Buddhists do not think of their devotion as prayer because they do not consider the Buddha a god. But some kinds of Buddhism, like Pure Land, uses many devotional elements such as prayer.

When Buddhists pray, they feel that it "releases the Buddha within," or the true nature that is trapped inside a person. Some Buddhists see this as a kind of meditation, others consider it as showing respect to the Buddha.

A Buddhist named Dr. Fernando once said:

"Prayer doesn't exist in (Theravada) Buddhism because there is no one to talk to. In my devotions, I say to myself 'To the best of my ability, I shall try to emulate the life of the Buddha.'"

Flags and wheels

In some Buddhist countries, flags are raised with the words of an important **mantra** written on them. When the wind blows the flag, they

Tibetan prayer wheels

believe the blessing of the mantra is released and the energy contained in the thought is carried in the wind. Similarly, some Buddhists use prayer wheels to release the prayers into the environment.

Beads and bells

Many Buddhists use **mala beads** to help them meditate. There are 108 mala beads on a string, which help the practitioner to focus on an object and to release interfering thoughts.

Some Buddhists use bells to help them. In Tibet, a bell is seen as a symbol of wisdom.

Some Buddhists may hold a **vajra** (a scepter or wand) while meditating. This is a symbol of the Buddha's power and the truth behind all things.

Repentance and forgiveness

One part of devotion that is important to Buddhists is repentance, or apologizing for things that they have done wrong. During the months from July to October, the Buddha arranged a retreat for his followers, where they could think through the ways in which they needed to change. Many Buddhists use this time today to think about the areas of their life that they could improve.

In Myanmar (Burma), Buddhists celebrate the festival of Thadingyut. This festival celebrates the Buddha's return from heaven to tell all people to forgive each other and themselves. Thadingyut takes place in the month of October, and is called the Festival of Lights. It is a time of great joy, and people take this opportunity to give thanks.

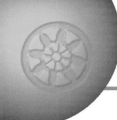

Meditation

In this section you will

- learn about the Buddhist practice of meditation as a way to develop self-understanding, and as a way to gain calm and insight;

- read about the use of mantras in Buddhism, and the Mani mantra in particular.

Thinking it through

If you get stuck on a math problem, you may need to think about it for quite a while before you come to a solution. If you are in an argument, you would be wise to think before

you speak! We often need time to think through things so that our actions will not result in destructive or negative consequences. Meditation, on the other hand, is a way to find inner calmness that does not involve "thinking."

Buddhist meditation

The Buddha had his experience of enlightenment as a result of meditation. For Buddhists today, meditation is a powerful technique to help them work with the mind in order to gain understanding. Meditation enables them to train the mind to make it fit, just as jogging enables a body to get fit. The following is how a Buddhist might meditate.

Solving a problem by thinking

Meditation has many aims. Meditation can help Buddhists realize the meaning of the great truths of the Buddha and enable them to gain awareness of things in their own lives that need changing and developing. Because it leads to clarity, understanding, and calm, meditation also leads to freedom from suffering. It is helpful to use some characteristics that the Buddha thought were supportive. These were called the **Brahma Viharas,** or "spiritual friends," and include the following:

1. **metta,** or loving kindness—being gentle and tender to all;

2. **karuna,** or compassion—an understanding and concern for others;

3. **mudita,** or sympathetic joy—showing delight in the success of others;

4. **upekkah,** or evenness of mind—showing a balanced approach to life.

Meditation can be practiced both alone and in groups at the local Buddhist center or temple.

Meditation is an important Buddhist practice.

Breathe in slowly through your nose and as you do so, feel relaxed. Use your breath as a focus of your attention so that your mind does not wander off with thoughts. As you breathe out, feel the tensions in your body leaving you. Try to concentrate on the rhythm of your breathing.

As you feel your breath, notice how thoughts and sensations arise in your mind. You may get caught up in these and lose awareness of your breath. When this happens, simply notice that you have drifted away from your focus and return to the breath. Meditation involves being fully aware of everything but getting caught up by nothing, so it is not the same as thinking. With practice, meditation can lead to a still, peaceful mind, relaxed but fully aware.

Mantras

For many Buddhists, chanting a phrase or mantra in their times of worship or meditation helps them greatly. Mantras are often given to individual Buddhists by Buddhist teachers. However, a common mantra, used by Tibetan Buddhists, is the Mani mantra.

Each day, Buddhists chant the words of the Mani mantra: "Om Mani Padme Hum." This comes from the Lotus Sutra. In English, it means, "Hail to the Jewel of the Lotus." According to Buddhist teaching, the Mani mantra is "the essence of all happiness, prosperity, and knowledge, and source of the great liberation."

Sometimes Buddhist mantras are written on prayer flags or on prayer wheels in Buddhist temples and holy places so that, symbolically, the wind can blow the peace of the mantras across the world.

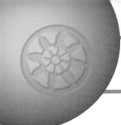

Buddhist Holy Places

In this section you will
- find out the importance of holy buildings to Buddhists and the symbolism attached to them;
- learn about rupas, found in Buddhist shrines.

Important places

Try to think about the places you have been to during your life. Perhaps you remember a vacation in a really beautiful place, which you really enjoyed. Or perhaps it was a visit to a historical museum that you enjoyed most.

The vihara

Buddhists, like other religious people, often visit important places where they go to pay respect. One name for such a place is the **vihara.**

A Buddhist vihara

The vihara is sometimes attached to a monastery but not always. The vihara contains a shrine room where Buddhists meet to meditate, pray, and celebrate important festivals.

In the shrine room, there are several important items. Often, the room is dominated by a statue of the Buddha, which is used as a focus of intention and a reminder of his teaching. There may be pictures of the Buddha and other important Buddhist figures in the room as well.

Often by the statue you will find flowers, incense sticks, and candles. The flowers are a symbol to remind the assembly that the Buddha taught that life is always changing. The incense sticks represent Dharma (truth) and are offered to show the intention to live a life of good deeds and truthfulness. The candle is a symbol of the wisdom and insight that can be found in the Buddha and the Dharma.

Other buildings

There are many other kinds of holy buildings in the Buddhist faith.

A stupa

A wat

A pagoda

People often call Buddhist places of worship temples but they have many other names too. In Thailand, Buddhists worship in a building called a **wat.**

A **stupa** is very special. Each stupa is shaped like a bell, because bells are used to call Buddhists to meditation. These buildings contain a relic from the Buddha or from an important Buddhist leader.

The temple in Kandy in Sri Lanka is said to contain Buddha's tooth (see page 36), and is a place of pilgrimage.

A **pagoda** is another type of building that is important to Buddhists. It is built in five sections. These remind Buddhists that the universe has five basic elements—earth, fire, water, wind, and space. Sometimes these buildings are also called **dagodas.**

Shrines at home

Not all meditation takes place in the temples or the viharas. Buddhists often set aside a space or even an entire room in their homes as places to pay respect and to meditate.

The Wimbledon Buddhist Temple

One very impressive building for Buddhist worship in England is the Wimbledon Buddhist Temple. This was built by the government of Thailand. A small community of monks regularly holds services there for people who work in the Embassy of Thailand in London.

Rupas

A **rupa** is an image of the Buddha, found in Buddhist shrines. The Buddha is normally shown in one of three positions: standing, sitting, or lying down. The Buddharupa will also show the Buddha holding his hands in one of the **mudras,** or hand positions, which symbolize different ways of being. For example, if the Buddha is shown sitting down with both hands raised forming circles with index finger and thumb touching, it shows that he is teaching.

Buddhist Scriptures

In this section you will

● find out about some of the most important holy writings to Buddhists;

● read and reflect upon some of the teachings from the Buddhist scriptures.

Preserving the past

There are many ways in which we learn about the past. Archaeologists may dig up artifacts such as pots, coins, and weapons from long ago. There are castles and other buildings that are still used today, but also tell us about the past. Yet one of the most important ways we can learn about the past is through the books that people in the past wrote.

The Three Baskets

The Buddha's teaching was passed down through the years and preserved in the chants of the Sangha.

The Buddha's followers did not originally think that it was important to write down the stories of the Buddha. Most scholars think that the first Buddhist holy books were written down about 500 years after the time of the Buddha.

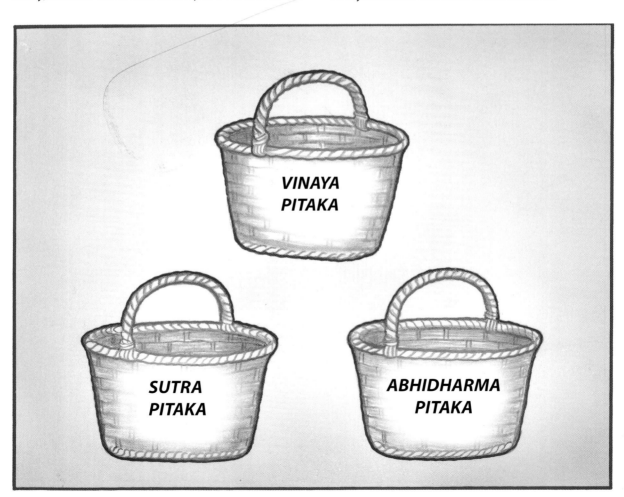

The Three Baskets

Before the books were written, the stories and teachings of the Buddha were passed down by word of mouth. People had to train their memories to remember important ideas because there were not as many opportunities to write or to store information. Many communities in these earlier times also relied on storytellers to keep traditional ideas alive.

In 30 B.C.E., a group of monks gathered on the island of Sri Lanka. They put together a book known as the **Tripitaka,** or the Three Baskets.

The Three Baskets are:

1. the **Vinaya Pitaka**— the rules that only monks and nuns have to follow and stories about how they were formed;

2. the **Sutra Pitaka**—a collection of teachings given by the Buddha;

3. the **Abidharma Pitaka**—texts that analyze and develop the ideas of Buddhist philosophy.

Other scriptures

According to Buddhist teachings, the Buddha had lived many other lifetimes as animals and other humans. There are a number of stories about these other lives, which have been collected together to form the **Jataka** tales. There are 540 Jataka tales in all.

The **Dharmapada** is another important scripture, because it brings together some of the Buddha's sayings (423 verses in total). Here is a selection:

"One should give up anger—one should abandon pride."

Verse 221

"Self-conquest is indeed far better than the conquest of others."

Verse 104

"Better than a thousand useless words is one single word that brings peace."

Verse 100

In India, in the first century C.E., Buddhists began to collect teachings from the time of the Buddha. The Chinese Buddhists began to collect their material a century later.

There are other important books in Buddhism that are developments of the Buddha's teachings. One example is the Tibetan *Book of the Dead.* This was written to help people prepare for their next life and to think about the consequences of the way they have lived.

Teachings from the Buddhist scriptures

Here are examples of some of the teachings found in the Buddhist scriptures:

"Though one man conquer a thousand times a thousand men in battle, he who conquers himself is the greatest warrior."

Dharmapada

"Victory breeds hatred. The defeated live in pain. Happily the peaceful live, giving up victory and defeat."

Dharmapada

"I preach the Dharma to all beings whether their intellect be inferior or superior, and their faculties be weak or strong."

Lotus Sutra

"The secret of health, both physical and mental, is not to mourn for the past, not to worry about the future and not to anticipate troubles but to live wisely and earnestly in the present."

Sutra Pitaka

The Festival of Wesak

In this section you will

● learn about the Buddhist festival of Wesak and its importance to Buddhist people;

● read about the festival of Hana Matsuri in Mahayana Buddhist countries.

Celebrations

It is very important that we have times to celebrate, times when we can have parties to mark important events. It may be New Year's or birthday, or when we see our team win an event.

We all need to enjoy the good things in life, to feel that life is worth living, and to show what we think is most important.

Wesak

Wesak (called "Buddha Day" by some Buddhists) is the most important festival of the Buddhist year. It celebrates the most important events in the life of the Buddha—his birth, his enlightenment, and when he died and entered into the state of **parinirvana**. Some Buddhists believe that all of these three things happened on the same day in different years. The celebration takes place at the time of the full moon in late May or June.

Washing the images of the Buddha

Wesak in Thailand

In Thailand, Wesak is a very important occasion. Many Buddhists visit a monastery on that day, taking with them flowers, a candle, and a stick of incense. The candle's lighted wick is a sign of wisdom, while the melted wax and the flowers are a sign that nothing is permanent. The incense represents truth and is a sign of devotion to the Buddha.

People may walk around a stupa three times, in order to show their commitment to following the Buddha, the Dharma, and the Sangha in their lives. Some water bodhi trees, to remind them that it was under such a tree that the Buddha came to understand the truth.

Houses are cleaned and statues of the Buddha are washed. Fish that have been caught days earlier are released back into the river to show how the Buddha's teaching brings freedom. Birds are often released from cages as another image of the freedom that Buddhists are celebrating.

Wesak in Sri Lanka

In Sri Lanka, huge paintings of events from the life of the Buddha are put on display. Lanterns are hung. Street performers such as acrobats and dancers perform.

It is a time to share the best things in life with other people, so often wayside stalls of food and drink are set up to help people who may have traveled long distances to come to the festival ceremonies.

Extra moral precepts

During the festival, Buddhists may decide to follow five more moral precepts. These are normally kept just by monks and nuns. They are:

- not eating after midday;

- not sleeping on a comfortable bed;

- not watching any form of entertainment, such as television;

- not wearing jewelry or perfume;

- not handling any money.

Hana Matsuri

In Japan, the birth of the Buddha is celebrated in the festival of Hana Matsuri, or "flower festival." Hana Matsuri takes place in the spring, and spring flowers are taken to shrines and used to decorate statues of the Buddha that show him as a child. Temples hold displays to illustrate stories about the Buddha's birth. Traditional dancing takes place, and people sell food in stalls in the streets.

Other Buddhist Festivals

In this section you will

● find out about the meaning and traditions attached to other important Buddhist festivals;

● read about the Buddhist festival of Vassa.

New Year

New Year is often an important celebration for both religious and nonreligious people. It enables people to reflect on what has happened in the past year, to take stock. It is also a time to think about the future. Some people make resolutions to change or improve themselves in the year ahead.

Songkran

In Thailand, New Year's doesn't take place on January 1, but in the middle of April. The festival of **Songkran** is a time to celebrate the new year.

Songkran is a festival that relies on water. Thai people splash each other with water as part of the celebration of a new beginning. There are colorful parades, boat races, masks, and dances. A princess of the festival is elected.

When the festival ends, Thai people put on new clothes. They also release into rivers fish they have previously caught, a symbol of the release that enlightenment brought to the Buddha.

Festival of the Tooth

The Festival of the Tooth takes place on the island of Sri Lanka. Buddhists believe that one of the Buddha's teeth has been kept in a specially built **stupa.** The tooth is kept inside a series of nested caskets and is not brought out until the festival takes place.

Songkran can get you very wet!

Elephants at the Festival of the Tooth

On the night of the full moon in August, there is a procession of elephants, led by one that is decked out in a golden costume.

The procession includes dancers, jugglers, and other street entertainers, as well as the monks who care for the casket.

Obon

Obon is a festival celebrated by Japanese Buddhists on July 13. It celebrates a time when the Buddha rescued the mother of one of his disciples from hell. It is a time to pay respects to ancestors, so Buddhists clean the graves of their departed relatives with water and also adorn them with flowers.

Prayers are offered for the dead relatives and then incense is burned in order to encourage their spirits to return to the world from which they came. At the end of the festival, a huge bonfire is lit at Mount Daimonjiyama outside the city of Kyoto.

Obon is a time to remember those who have died.

The festival of Vassa

Another important Buddhist festival is the festival of Vassa. This takes place in the month of August, and celebrates the time when the Buddha first started sharing his teaching at the Deer Park in Benares in India. At the beginning of the festival of Vassa, monks and nuns go to their monasteries for a time of teaching.

In some countries at Vassa, Buddhist boys are dressed up as the young Siddhartha and take part in a procession that ends in the local temple or vihara. They may at this point have their heads shaved and enter the monastery. The monks may be offered bowls and new robes by Buddhists in the local area as a mark of respect for the work they do in heading the religious life of the community.

Buddhist Pilgrimage

In this section you will
- find out about some of the important places of pilgrimage for Buddhists;
- read about places in Tibet that Buddhist pilgrims like to visit.

Places of Buddhist pilgrimage

A vacation place for rest and relaxation

Special places

People like to visit special places. When we go on such trips, we often do so not for rest and relaxation but because the places have an important meaning for us.

Lumbini Grove

"The place…at which the devoted person can say,'Here the Buddha was born' is a spot to be visited with feelings of reverence."

The Buddha was born in Lumbini Grove in Nepal. When he was born, Buddhists believe that the earth was filled with light and shook in expectation. He was brought up in the area. The great Buddhist King Asoka built a pillar to point out that it was here the Buddha was born.

Bodh Gaya

"The place…at which the devoted person can say,'Here the Buddha attained supreme and highest wisdom' is a spot to be visited with feelings of reverence."

At Bodh Gaya, sitting beneath a bodhi tree, Siddhartha Gautama received the enlightenment that led him to become the Buddha. A bodhi tree grows today in the spot where Buddhists believe the first one was located. The tree is adorned with prayer flags.

Pilgrims come to the tree to worship and to meditate. There are many temples in the area.

A shrine near the bodhi tree at Bodh Gaya

Sarnath

"The place,…at which the devoted person can say, 'Here the wheel of the Dharma was set in motion by the Buddha' is a spot to be visited with feelings of reverence."

It was at the Deer Park in **Sarnath** that the Buddha preached his first sermon, in which he explained his teachings on the meaning of and solution to suffering. The holy men, who had once abandoned him, became his first disciples.

Kushingara

"The place,…at which the devoted person can say, 'Here the Buddha passed finally away' is a spot to be visited with feelings of reverence."

It was at the house of Chunda that the Buddha ate the food that would lead to his death. For Buddhists, this is a place of great holiness as it was here that the Buddha completed his personal journey to **nirvana.**

Pilgrimage to Tibet

There are many places of pilgrimage for Buddhists across Asia, including Tibet. Not all of them are directly connected with the life of the Buddha himself.

For example, many people go on pilgrimage to Tibet to see the temple and cave where the founder of Tibetan Buddhism, Padmasambhava, and his friend, Yeshe Tsogyal, meditated. Padmasambhava was said to have spent seven years in the cave meditating.

Another place that Buddhist pilgrims like to visit in Tibet is Mount Kailash. Many believe this to be the center of the universe because the four great rivers of the area— the Ganges, the Indus, the Brahmaputra, and the Karnali—all meet at this point. The pilgrims walk 32 miles (50 km) around the base of Mount Kailash. People are not allowed to climb the mountain; the only person ever to have been to the top of Mount Kailash was a Tibetan Buddhist in the 11th century C.E.

Living in a Monastery

Joining a monastery

There are Buddhist monasteries all across the world, including in the United States.

In some Buddhist countries, such as Thailand, a young boy may become a monk for a short time in his childhood as a way of getting good karma for himself and his family. It is also a very good way of getting an education, because the monasteries are the main places to learn in many Asian countries.

If he decides to stay in the monastery, the boy will go to a special school in the monastery. If he stays long enough to want to become a full adult member of the community, he will go through two stages before he gets to be a monk.

1 as a **shramanera**—at this stage, he is what is known as a novice and is on probation to see if it is a good idea for him to stay;

A boy's head is shaved as he joins a monastery.

2 as a **bhikshu**—he has to be at least 20 before he can reach this stage. To become a bhiksu is to make the formal promise to stay a monk for the rest of your life.

There are many tests that a person has to go through before being fully accepted into the life of the monastery.

What effect does joining the monastery have?

Having decided to become an ordained monk, the candidate will have his head and beard shaved. To remove hair is a sign that the monk is prepared to put aside vanity and to realize that all things are subject to change and that nothing is permanent.

When he has received his robe from the community, he will be given an alms bowl. In Thailand he may be given sandals, needle and thread, a string of beads, a razor, an umbrella, and a net to strain out insects from his drinking water. In some monasteries, a monk owns his own robe and his bowl, though he may be given the use of other items.

At the ceremony, five monks have to mark out the boundaries of the monastery. Then the candidate kneels in front of the senior monk, normally called the abbot.

The candidate asks the abbot for permission to become a member. The abbot recites a meditation about how all human life is perishable. The candidate asks for forgiveness, promises that he will not boast, that he is committed to the Buddha, Dharma, and the Sangha, and that he will follow the rules of the monastery.

The candidate has to state that his parents have accepted his calling, that he is a free man, free from debt and employment, and that he is

Life in a monastery

Monks may live in forest dwellings or help to run the local **vihara.** If their monastery is large, they may well run a school. In England, some monasteries are located in large houses in the country, like the one pictured, at Chithurst in Sussex.

In several countries, there are also shared and separate monasteries for nuns. Nuns have to follow even more rules than the monks do.

Things a monk may own

human and male. He will be given a Buddhist name by the abbot, normally one that suggests a quality that he could develop.

Chithurst Monastery in Sussex, England

Thich Nhat Hanh

Thich Nhat Hanh (pronounced Tick-Naught-Han) is a Buddhist monk from Vietnam who was nominated for the Nobel Peace Prize by Martin Luther King, Jr. in 1967. He became a monk when he was 16 years old. When he was 40 years old, he was forced to leave his home country because the government objected to the nonviolent resistance he led against the Vietnam War in the 1960s.

Thich Nhat Hanh now lives in a small Buddhist community of 30 monks and nuns in France, where he works with refugees from across the world and leads retreats on peacemaking. He has established a movement, called "engaged Buddhism," which combines meditation with nonviolent civil disobedience (protest).

Thich Nhat Hanh wrote, "Every day we do things that have to do with peace. If we are aware of our life… our way of looking at things, we will know how to make peace right in the moment we are alive."

Being in a Community

In this section you will

● learn more about what it means to belong to a monastery and why monasteries are still important to Buddhist people today;

● read about Buddhist nuns and how their communities began.

Following the rules

Many people find following rules very difficult. Some people even say that rules are made to be broken.

Try playing a board game or a tennis match without rules, and it just won't work. If a person were to ignore rules when he or she were driving a car, someone would soon get hurt.

We may not like rules but we might find that we often need them to keep us safe or to help us enjoy the best of life.

The intentions of a monastery

Buddhists have to follow the Five Moral Precepts, but monks and nuns are expected to follow not only these, but others as well. These include:

1. not to eat after midday;

2. not to sing, dance, or be entertained;

3. not to wear jewelry or perfume, or beautify themselves;

4. not to sleep in a high or broad bed;

5. not to handle money.

Some of the things a monk has to give up

The **Vinaya**, or rules, are followed voluntarily because Buddhism is a personal training system based on restraint and giving up things rather than a system to keep monks or nuns in line. The reason for the training is to be free from desire. The more simple the lifestyle without luxury— with only food, shelter, and medicine—the less indulgence in feelings of desire.

By wearing jewelry, perfume, or flowers, the monks and nuns would be attracting attention to themselves. By sleeping on a simple bed, they show that they can give up comfort.

All monks are given alms bowls, but they are not allowed to receive money directly. The alms bowls are where Buddhists put gifts of food. Almsgivers can also offer practical support for the work of the local monastery.

Each monastery may have its own set of rules. For example, the Theravada monks try to follow 227 rules, the nuns, 311. The Zen or Tibetan Vinaya may have different guidelines.

The Chithurst monastery in England stresses the value of the following precepts among lay Buddhists and the monastic community, which extends these to 227 precepts. The Five Moral Precepts are:

1 *to avoid taking life*—not to hurt a living thing, be it human or animal;

2 *to avoid taking what is not given*—stealing is strictly forbidden;

3 *to avoid sexual misconduct*—celibacy for monks means that they are not to take part in any sexual behavior;

4 *to avoid speaking falsely*—not to speak in a way that is offensive or proud;

5 *to avoid drink and drugs that can cloud the mind*—to refrain from taking drugs and alcohol that could hinder clear-mindedness.

Daily life in the monastery

At the Chithurst monastery, the day begins at 5:00 A.M. with chanting and meditation sessions. There is time for breakfast and performing some morning duties before the next meditation at 7:30 A.M. There is a meeting to decide on the morning and afternoon jobs to be done before the monks sit down for the main and only meal of the day. This is served at 10:30 A.M. and is followed by a rest time, then by more tasks. In the afternoon, there is a cup of tea and then the monks retire at 9:00 P.M. On some evenings chanting and meditation last through the night.

Buddhist nuns

There are Buddhist monks and nuns all over the world today, although monks outnumber nuns considerably. But when did the order, or community, of Buddhist nuns first become established? There are different versions of events in Buddhist literature. One story suggests that Kisa Gotami was the first Buddhist nun, but another story tells that Mahaprajapati (the Buddha's stepmother) was the founder of the order.

In the story that says that Mahaprajapati was the first nun, the Buddha's assistant, Ananda, argued with the Buddha about the need to establish an order of nuns. When the Buddha agreed to this, the story goes, he added rules for the nuns that said they had to obey the monks. Many Buddhists, however, believe that this story was told by people after the time of the Buddha. These people, they claim, had become worried about the fact that the Buddha himself often seemed to think that differences between the sexes do not matter. In India at the time, women did not have the same status as men, and so the Buddha's teaching challenged people in an important way.

Birth

In this section you will

● find out about the way some Buddhists celebrate the birth of children and learn about the ideas attached to these ceremonies;

● read about the Pravrajya ceremony.

Birthdays

Birthdays can be very important to all of us. Most of us love to receive presents and cards, to know that other people have given us signs that they love and care for us.

Birth ceremonies in Buddhism

Buddhists often mark the birth of a child with what is called a birth blessing. Here, the child is given a blessing on entering the world but its Buddhist name as a lay person or an adult will be given later.

In some countries, such as Myanmar (Burma), the family will gather at the birth of a child to celebrate. They will give the child a cradle and put gifts in it.

The gifts are those considered to be helpful for the child. If the child is a boy, the presents are normally things such as books and tools—for example, a hammer. If the child is a girl, she may be given a needle and some thread.

Birthdays can be important celebrations

A child is very precious to its parents.

In **Theravada** countries, monks may sprinkle the child with water, symbolizing a wish for the child to be blessed in the future. A wax candle may be dripped into some water, as a sign that the child belongs to the four elements of earth, air, fire, and water.

Importance of family life for the Buddha

The Buddha believed that family life was very important to help us grow as people.

He compared the family to a group of trees in the forest. They are able to support each other and give each other protection against the wind. We need our families to help us, he said.

When a child is about a month old, in some Buddhist countries, his or her hair might be shaved off, because some Buddhists believe that hair links the child back to the bad **karma** of its previous life. It is a way of saying that a new life is a new start and that the problems of the past should be forgotten to make a better future possible. Other Buddhists think that this is just a superstition based on a mistaken interpretation of Buddhist ideas.

Monks are invited to the ceremony. They may be asked to give the child a name that reflects the qualities that the child might aspire to. Or they may name the child after a great Buddhist from the past. Monks will normally chant scriptures on behalf of the child.

In Thailand, the parents will often give the monks food as a gift in order to win good karma for the child. In other countries, food is given to the monks to recognize that their teaching nourishes the spiritual life.

In some Buddhist countries, a sacred thread may be wound around the wrist of the child as a sign inviting blessing.

The Pravrajya ceremony

In Myanmar (Burma), it is very common for Buddhist boys to join a monastery when they are only ten years old, or even younger. This gives them the opportunity to gain good karma, as well as a good education. Some of the boys stay on to become monks. The Pravrajya ceremony takes place at this stage.

During the Pravrajya ceremony, the boy dresses up as a prince and acts out the story of how Siddhartha Gautama left his palace to seek enlightenment. The boy rides on a donkey or pony, leading a procession through the streets until he reaches the monastery. Here, he removes his fine clothes and replaces them with an orange robe. His hair and his eyebrows are shaved off. The boy then promises to obey ten moral precepts followed by monks, and he is given a new name. His family may give the boy gifts, such as a spare robe or an alms bowl.

Marriage

In this section you will
● learn about the importance of marriage to Buddhists, including its symbolic elements;
● read and reflect upon some of the vows and blessings used in weddings.

Committed for life?

Marriage, for many people, is a way of publicly saying before your family, friends, the community, and, for some, before God, that you intend to stay together in a loving relationship.

Marriage in Buddhist countries

Buddhist countries differ in their marriage customs, but there are some things that are common to all of them.

In some, but not all, Buddhist countries, marriages are arranged by parents. In other Buddhist countries, marriage is a result of the couple's own personal choice.

In a country like Thailand, the wedding takes place in the bride's home, where monks will be invited to bless the couple and to recite scriptures to encourage them. Monks do not actually perform the marriage ceremony, which may be done by a relative, such as the uncle of the bride.

The couple stands on a special platform called a **purowa**, which is decorated with white flowers. During the ceremony, the couple exchange rings, and vows are made by each partner. A silk scarf is wrapped around their hands as a way of saying that they have been joined together as husband and wife.

In **Theravada** Buddhist countries, a thread of cotton is passed around the temple where the marriage is to take place. Two pieces of the

A Buddhist wedding

A monk can bless the newly married couple

thread will then be cut. A monk wraps one around the wrist of the bridegroom and then the bridegroom is handed the other thread. He then winds this around the wrist of his bride, since monks are not allowed to touch a woman as part of their monastic vows.

It is the tradition that after the wedding ceremonies, a large feast is supplied by the family and friends.

In order for the new relationship to get off to a good start, the couple or their parents make a gift of food to the monks as a way of earning good **karma** and also to support the monks.

Marriage vows and blessings

During a Buddhist marriage ceremony, the bride and bridegroom are expected to recite vows taken from the Sigalovada Sutra, part of the Buddhist scriptures.

The bridegroom says: "Toward my wife, I undertake to love and respect her, be kind and considerate, be faithful, delegate domestic management, provide gifts to please her."

The bride says: "Toward my husband, I undertake to perform my household duties efficiently, be hospitable to my in-laws and friends of my husband, be faithful, protect and invest our earnings, discharge my responsibilities lovingly and conscientiously."

After this, the parents recite the Mangala Sutra and the Jayamangala Gatha, also part of the Buddhist scriptures, to bless the couple. The Mangala Sutra sets out those blessings that are considered to be the greatest possible blessings. The Jayamangala Gatha calls on the gods to bless the newlyweds.

Death

In this section you will

● learn about the Buddhist beliefs surrounding death and how Buddhists mark the passing of a person;

● reflect on how to deal with questions of grief and bereavement.

The hard truth

We know that we will all die, but it is still hard to know how to deal with our grief when a loved one dies. Different religions have varying beliefs about death and different practices surrounding it, and most offer ways to give solace to the survivors.

A Buddhist cemetery

A Buddhist funeral procession in Myanmar (Burma)

Buddhist funerals

Buddhist funerals are not the same worldwide.

In Sri Lanka, funeral ceremonies are not times of mourning but can become an opportunity to improve the **karma** of the dead as they move to the next life.

The body is washed and then the hands are clasped together. A thread is wound around the deceased's hands as a sign of three things that tie a person to this world—money, marriage, and children.

Several items are placed in the coffin:

1. a small ladder, which will enable the mind of the deceased to leave the body behind;

2. flowers and incense, which are signs that life is impermanent and leads only surely to death;

3. a small set of flags, which will help the dead person to arrive in the heavens.

The funeral normally takes place in a local monastery. The body is then cremated on a pyre. A monk later gathers the ashes of the deceased and recites a scripture reminding the relatives how short life is.

Some of the bones of the deceased may be placed in a half-circle to show the reality of life, and then turned to the east to symbolize death. The pieces of bone and ash are then collected and buried in an urn. If the person who has died was felt to be especially holy, he or she may have a relic preserved in a **stupa.**

Funerals in Mahayana countries

In countries such as China, Taiwan, and Korea, special attention is given to honoring dead ancestors, reflecting the influence of Confucianism. When a person dies, a monk places a memorial tablet on the family shrine in the home of the person who has died.

The monk then applies "last water" to the deceased and washes the body.

Friends and neighbors often celebrate with a vegetarian meal. They also burn incense at the graveyard.

Families continue to mourn formally after the death of their relative as a way of securing good karma for the person who has died. Relatives may also give gifts to the monks for their support during this time.

One Buddhist writer has written:

No weeping, nor yet sorrowing,
Nor any kind of mourning aids,
Departed one, whose kin remain,
(Unhelped by their action) thus.

From *Minor Readings* by Bhikkhu Naranoni

Chinese Buddhist funerals

In a Chinese Buddhist family, when a person dies, the funeral ceremony can last up to 49 days. The first seven days are the most important, although the number of days given to the ceremony will depend on how rich the bereaved family is. Prayers are said every day for the whole 49 days if the family can afford it; if not, the period may be shortened to three to seven days. Normally, the daughters of the family are expected to pay for the cost of the funeral ceremony.

Chinese Buddhists follow the Mahayana Buddhist tradition, so they believe that between the death and rebirth of a person there is a time when that person is in a state of waiting. It is important, during this waiting time, for the family to try to earn good karma for the dead relative by praying and doing good works.

The Environment

In this section you will

- find out the key ideas that Buddhists hold about the environment;
- reflect on the important issues concerning the environment and how we can improve things.

What a wonderful world

We live in a beautiful world, but it has often been damaged by the actions of human beings. For example, the aerosols we have used in the past have contributed to the greenhouse effect, which has led to climate change.

Oil spills from tankers have often ruined large areas of the ocean and coastline and caused the death of many birds and other forms of wildlife.

Humans have often made decisions that have made the world a less than beautiful place.

Do no harm

Buddhists believe that they should do no harm to any living thing. This idea is called **ahimsa.** For many Buddhists, it means that they do all they can to avoid killing any form of life.

Some monks, for example, are given a strainer so that they will not swallow insects by mistake when drinking.

Pollution can damage the earth.

One Buddhist left a trail of sugar to encourage some ants to leave the kitchen rather than using ant poison that would have killed them.

Who made the earth?

Buddhists say they do not believe in a creator god who made the planet because they have no first-hand experience of such a god. But they do not deny a creator god, either. They believe in creating a better world by making wise choices and doing no harm throughout their lives.

Karma

As we have seen, Buddhists believe that all actions have consequences. The force of these actions and consequences is known as karma. If we choose to live in a way that damages others, we damage the planet as well, and we create bad karma for ourselves.

The environment will also be affected by the whole of humanity, so people need to encourage governments and other groups that work for the environment.

"As the bee takes the essence of a flower and flies around without destroying its beauty and perfume, so let the sage (the wise person) wander in this life."

Dharmapada 49

Buddhist care for the environment

Good Buddhists do not abuse the environment. If they have to take from the environment, then they also put things back into it. For example, if a tree were cut down, a Buddhist would plant a tree to replace it.

Buddhists teach that all of nature is interconnected and that we need to make sure that we care for it, for we are an important part of it.

Earth Sangha

Many Buddhists are involved in environmental protection. One such group is the Earth Sangha in the United States. They try to apply the teachings of Buddhism to the issues of the environment. They run teaching days, which help people to live lives that reflect the idea of sustainability; that is, that what you take out of the earth you should try to put back in: you should plant a tree to replace one used to make a table.

The Earth Sangha teaches that we are all part of one earth and that we have a responsibility to care for all things in nature. They believe that there is a strong link between Buddhism and environmentalism. For example, because one of the aims of Buddhism is clarity of mind—and, following from this, personal health—then it is logical for Buddhists also to be concerned with environmental health. Buddhists, above all, are on a search to learn about themselves, and part of this learning can come from the personal choices they make regarding the environment. Buddhism is a religion of compassion, and Buddhists believe this compassion should reach out to include all creatures and the entire earth.

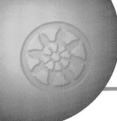

Wealth and Poverty

In this section you will

● find out about Buddhist views on wealth and poverty;

● read and reflect on a Buddhist's teaching about suffering.

One world?

Economists (people who study how money is made and the consequences of the way it is spent) say that the world could be divided into two groups:

1 the developed nations—the richest countries in the world, including the United States, Japan, Germany, Britain, and France;

2 the developing nations—poor nations that are said to be developing rather than rich or wealthy.

In the developing nations, thousands of children die of hunger every day. Millions also die of disease before their fifth birthday because they have inadequate health care.

Buddhist teaching on wealth and poverty

Siddhartha was born into great wealth, but he chose to live the life of the poor holy men he had encountered on his visits to the city.

He realized that neither poverty nor riches, neither pleasure nor pain was the way to achieve the truth he sought.

The Buddha taught that what was necessary was a Middle Way between the two extremes. So a Buddhist today would argue that we need a balance—enough food for everyone's needs, but not enough to satisfy greed.

Buddhism teaches care of the poor.

The Buddha shows compassion.

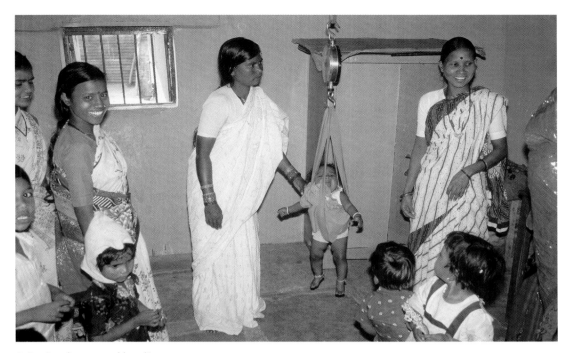

Bringing hope and healing

The Buddha also taught that "Desire leads to pain." We should think about those who are the victims of the consumption of the rich nations. We are all part of the one world and we need to acknowledge it. Buddhists believe that people will never find happiness through the endless acquisition of money and possessions.

Engaged Buddhism

The Buddhist monk Thich Nhat Hanh from Vietnam encouraged Buddhists to think about the consequences of their actions. Buddhism is a way of engaging with life, and its ultimate aim is to find peace within. This enables Buddhists to care for themselves and for others. By being aware of their intentions, for example, to help or not to help a person, Buddhists believe that good or bad karma will result.

Many Buddhists in Britain, for example, support the Karuna Trust, an organization that works with the poorest people in the world, trying to make sure they are fed and cared for. It also tries to help in the long-term development of the country.

Wealth and suffering

The Vietnamese Buddhist monk and political activist Thich Nhat Hanh has written on the subject of possessions, wealth, and our responsibility to those less fortunate than ourselves:

"Do not accumulate wealth while millions are hungry. Do not take the aim of your life as fame, wealth, profit, or sensual pleasure. Live simply and share time, energy, and material resources with those who are in need."

"Possess nothing that should belong to others. Respect the property of others but prevent others from enriching themselves from human suffering or the suffering of other human beings."

"Do not avoid contact with suffering or close your eyes before suffering. Do not lose awareness of the existence of suffering in the life of the world...."

Racism

In this section you will

● find out about the Buddhist teaching on racism and prejudice;

● read and reflect upon Buddhist quotations about equality.

All the same?

Many people experience some form of name calling or bullying when they are in school. There is something about human nature that seems to make some of us sometimes pick on those who are different from us.

A stereotype is a mental picture of a group of people that portrays all the members of the group as behaving the same way, for example, "All teenagers are trouble!"

Many people have prejudices, that is, they make a negative judgment of people or groups before they know anything about them.

Some people may discriminate against others on the basis of these prejudgments. For example, an employer might refuse to hire a woman or someone from a racial minority. Although the law bans this kind of behavior, it still happens in some places.

How a Buddhist sees racism

Buddhism teaches that racism is unskillful for a number of reasons. The Buddha talked of three poisons that could cloud the mind. These include ignorance and hatred, both of which contribute to racism. In the Eightfold Path, he taught the need to follow the way of Right Understanding. To judge people by the color of their skin or the birthplace of their parents leads to ignorance and suffering. Buddhists believe that

Stereotyping: forming a false mental picture of what other people are like

Buddhism teaches compassion and love.

judging people keeps one from finding the truth because judging fixes the mind in an attitude that prevents understanding. The part of the path that encourages Right Awareness also leads Buddhists away from being obsessed with themselves and helps them to think about others.

The part of the path that encourages Right Speech does the same—it leads Buddhist believers away from being obsessed with themselves and makes them think about others. Buddhists try never to talk in a proud or dismissive way.

In the Four Noble Truths, the Buddha taught that there was no such thing as a self. To be a racist is to claim that one self is better than another. This attitude narrowly defines a person and does not allow for understanding. Buddhism urges its followers to develop loving kindness (**metta**) toward all other living things.

Equality for all

The following quotations state the need to respect all people, leaving no room for racism.

"Whenever I meet even a foreigner I always have the same feeling that I am meeting another member of the human family."

The Dalai Lama

"Let no one… despise any being in any state; let none by anger or hatred wish harm to another. Even as a mother at the risk of her life watches over and protects her only child, so with a boundless mind one should cherish all living things, suffusing love over the entire world, above, below, and all around, without limit…."

From the Metta Sutra

55

In this section you will

● learn about the life and teaching of the Dalai Lama and come to understand why he is a very important figure for Buddhists today;

● read about the work undertaken by Richard Gere to support Tibet.

A special boy

In Tibet, the Buddhist community has been led by a leader with the title **Dalai Lama.** The Dalai Lama is believed to be the reincarnation of a very sacred **Bodhisattva,** an enlightened being who chooses to continue to be reborn in order to help others to reach the truth.

In 1940, a young boy called Tenzin Gyasto was declared to be the new Dalai Lama. He was made both religious leader and head of the country. When he was first appointed, he was so young that adults had to help him rule.

The Chinese invasion

In 1950, the Chinese invaded Tibet and declared that it would now become a province, or part, of China. The Chinese gradually took control of the country. In the capital city of Lhasa, many Tibetans rebelled against the Chinese, which led to a crackdown and the execution of many Tibetans.

The Dalai Lama decided to flee across the border to India, because he believed that he could best help the cause of the Tibetan people by arguing their case from a free country. He realized that he would face either house arrest or execution if he stayed in his country.

The Chinese increasingly attacked the monasteries in Tibet. They destroyed holy books and would not tolerate dissent. They believed that they were freeing the Tibetans from years of pointless, evil traditions. By the time the Chinese leader, Chairman Mao, died in 1976, much of Lhasa was destroyed.

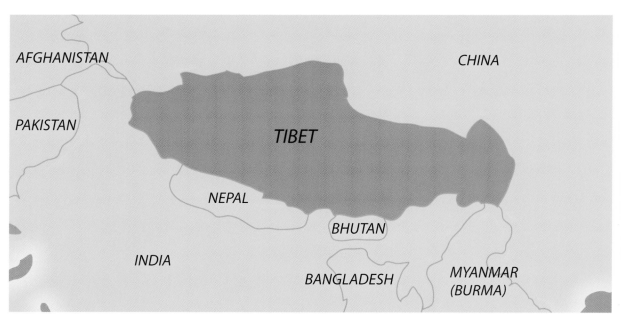

Tibet today

The Dalai Lama

The Dalai Lama has written:

"Today we are so interdependent, so closely interconnected that without a sense of universal responsibility, a feeling of universal brotherhood and sisterhood, and an understanding and belief that we are all part of one human family, we cannot hope to overcome the damage to our existence—let alone bring peace and happiness."

One person who has been greatly influenced by the Dalai Lama is the film actor Richard Gere. He established the Gere Foundation and has organized public events to highlight the problems Tibet is having.

A man of peace

The Dalai Lama is a man committed to peace and, although his country has been occupied, he refuses to advocate a violent response to what has happened. He has also been prepared to listen to the Chinese and has said that their political beliefs and those of Buddhism do not have to be at war with each other. His work has taken him across the world, speaking on behalf of the Tibetan people and calling for peace in the world.

Richard Gere

One person who is very concerned with the situation in Tibet and with helping the work of the Dalai Lama is the Hollywood movie actor, Richard Gere. Famous for movies such as *Pretty Woman*, Richard Gere became a Buddhist in the late 1970s, and has committed himself to **meditating** daily.

Gere has used his fame to help to publicize the problems of Tibet. He has set up Tibet House in New York, as well as the Gere Foundation. Tibet House is dedicated to the belief that the wisdom and arts of all countries enrich the entire world. Tibet House introduces people to Tibetan culture, with the aim of inspiring people to save Tibet from Chinese rule. The Gere Foundation provides practical aid to those who are working toward this goal.

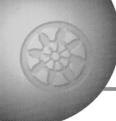

A monk's tale

Ajahn Sumedho is the leader of a group of Buddhist monks in the Theravadan tradition with monasteries in Great Britain, Italy, Switzerland, Thailand, North America, New Zealand, and Australia. Ajahn Sumedho was born Robert Jackson in Seattle in 1934.

Although brought up a Christian, he became more and more interested in the ideas and religion of the Far East. In 1963, he completed a doctorate in Far Eastern Studies and then decided to work as a teacher in Borneo.

Ajahn Sumedho

On a visit to Thailand in 1966, he decided to become an ordained monk of the order run by Ajahn Chah. In 1976, he was appointed the leader of the British Sangha.

Sumedho has written in his autobiography about the importance of Buddhist practice in helping him to understand how the world works. He wrote:

"The mind is like a mirror; it has the ability to reflect things. Mirrors reflect anything—beautiful or ugly, good or bad. And those things do not harm the mirror."

"We observe, 'This is how our lives have to be.' Then we wisely use what we have, learn from it, and free ourself from the narrow limits of self and mortality."

A politician's story

In 1989, Aung San Suu Kyi was elected as the leader of Myanmar (Burma) by 80 percent of the voters. Despite the fact that she won by such a large margin, the army stopped her from taking power by placing her under house arrest. They ruled that the election results did not count and that they were still in power. Aung San Suu Kyi had campaigned to remove corruption from the army and to make sure that no one would be abused by anyone in the army.

Her political party, the National League for Democracy, was banned. She was unable to leave the country, even when her husband died of cancer in her adopted country, Britain, in 1999.

Aung San Suu Kyi

As a Buddhist, Aung San Suu Kyi has told her party and her people that they must try to get the army to accept the result of the 1989 election by using nonviolent protest. She had learned from the example of the Hindu Indian leader, Mahatma Gandhi and the Christian civil rights leader, Martin Luther King, Jr. She has organized sit-ins and other protests promoting peace and democracy.

Facts about Myanmar (Burma)

- Buddhists make up 89 percent of the population. Muslims and Christians each make up 4 percent of the population.

- Myanmar is very rich in jewels, such as rubies; in metals, such as silver and lead; and in oil and gas.

Buddhism in the West

In recent years, Buddhism, which started as an Eastern religion, has become popular in Western countries, too. In the United States, there are more than 400,000 Buddhists. In Britain, there are about 135,000 Buddhists.

What is it that attracts Western people to Buddhism? One attraction may be that Westerners believe Buddhism to be a very tolerant religion. Buddhism ties in with a number of modern Western ideals, especially the desire to protect the environment and live in peace. And because many people have moved away from a traditional belief in God, Buddhism allows them to practice spirituality without the need for a god.

Glossary

Abhidharma Pitaka third of the three principal sections of the canon of basic scripture. It is a systematic, philosophical, and psychological treatment of the teachings given in the Sutra Pitaka

Ahimsa principle of pursuing harmlessness to all living creatures

Ananda Buddha's successor in leading the Buddhist community

Ascetic one who practices asceticism

Asceticism belief that by depriving the body of comforts you will get to spiritual truth

Avalokitesvara Bodhisattva representing perfect compassion

Bhikshu fully ordained Buddhist monk

Bodh Gaya place where Buddha became enlightened while sitting under the Bodhi Tree

Bodhisattva being destined for enlightenment, who postpones final attainment of Buddhahood in order to help living beings

Brahma Viharas four sublime states: loving kindness, compassion, sympathetic joy, and evenness of mind

Buddha Awakened or Enlightened One

Buddhism religion taught by the Buddha

Channa chariot driver who took Siddhartha to the city and to the forest

Chunda owner of the house where the Buddha ate what poisoned and killed him

Dalai Lama spiritual and temporal leader of the Tibetan people

Dana generosity, giving, gift

Dharmapada famous scripture of 423 verses

Dharma Buddha's teaching. Dharma means "universal truth"

Dhyana concentration

Eightfold Path principles to be followed to reach nirvana, as suggested by the Buddha. They will lead to freedom from the idea of the self

Engaged Buddhism idea that Buddhism should engage with the political and social questions of the world

Enlightenment experience of understanding what is true and what is not, to find the path to nirvana

Five Moral Precepts five moral intentions that Buddhists try to live their lives by

Four Noble Truths the teaching of the Buddha on suffering, its causes, and its solutions

Jataka tales told of the Buddha's many rebirths

Karma effect of intentional actions on one's circumstances in this and future lives. The Buddha's insistence that the effect depends on volition marks the Buddhist treatment of karma as different from the Hindu understanding of karma.

Karuna compassion

Kisagotami female follower of the Buddha, believed by many to have formed an order of Buddhist nuns

Kshanti patience

Kushingara place where the Buddha died

Lotus flower symbol of enlightenment

Lotus Sutra key teaching of the Buddha

Lumbini Grove place where according to legend the Buddha was born

Mahayana Buddhism one of the three main branches of Buddhism. Stresses the importance of Bodhisattvas

Maitreya a Bodhisattva who will bring a golden age in the future

Mala beads string of 108 beads used by some Buddhists to help in meditation

Mandalas images, often made of sand, that help Buddhists realize the changing and impermanent nature of life

Mantra words used by Buddhists during meditation and devotion

Mara devil-like figure who tried to confuse and tempt Siddhartha to stop him from becoming the Buddha

Meditation Mental practice of detached observation, to cultivate peaceful awareness of the moment and help to reach enlightenment

Metta loving kindness

Middle Way Buddha's teaching that the balance between self-indulgence and self-denial in life is necessary for enlightenment

Mudita sympathetic joy

Mudra hand position symbolizing a way of being

Nagasena Buddhist thinker who compared the self to a chariot

Nirvana state of secure, perfect peace that follows the extinction of the fires of greed, hatred, and ignorance. A key Buddhist term

Obon Japanese Buddhist festival in remembrance of the dead

Pagoda (dagoda) Buddhist religious building designed on five levels to show the nature of the universe as made of five elements

Pali Canon collected scriptures of Buddhism

Parinirvana state of bliss entered into by the Buddha on his death

Pitaka "basket," collection of scriptures

Prajna wisdom

Purowa platform that Buddhist couples stand on during marriage ceremonies

Rahula son of Siddhartha Gautama. His name means "chain"

Rupa image of the Buddha

Shramanera Buddhist novice monk

Sangha community, assembly.

Sarnath place where, in the Deer Park, Buddha delivered his first sermon after being enlightened

Siddhartha Gautama birth name of the historical Buddha

Sila morality

Skillful/Unskillful moral action that is either right, done with good intention (skillful) and producing good results; or inappropriate or wrong, done with bad intention (unskillful) and producing bad results

Songkran Thai Buddhist new year festival

Stupa religious building that contains a sacred relic of the Buddha or of an important Buddhist

Sutra Pitaka second of the three collections—principally of teachings—that make up the canon of basic scripture

Tara Bodhisattva who helps in enlightenment

Theravada "way of the elders," a principal branchof Buddhism, established in Sri Lanka and Southeast Asia. Also found in the West

Three Refuges three most important things in Buddhism: the Buddha, the Dharma (teaching), and the Sangha (the Buddhist community)

Tripitaka "three baskets," a threefold collection of texts (Vinaya, Sutra, Abhidharma)

Trikaya Buddhist teaching that the Buddha has three bodies

Upekkha serenity

Vajrayana a main branch of Buddhism

Vajra scepter or wand, a symbol of truth, used in some Buddhist prayer

Vihara dwelling place, monastery

Vinaya Pitaka first of the three collections of the canon of basic scripture, containing mostly the discipline for monks and nuns, with many stories and some teaching

Virya energy needed to progress on the path to enlightenment

Wat term for a Buddhist temple in Thailand

Wesak Buddha Day. Name of a festival and a month. On the full moon of Wesak (in May or June), the birth, enlightenment, and passing away of the Buddha took place, although some schools, such as Zen buddhism, celebrate only the birth at this time.

Wheel of life symbol used to explain how humans are trapped into suffering by the fact of existence. Sometimes shown with six spokes, but often shown with eight spokes, to show that following the eightfold path will help people escape from this life cycle.

Yashodhara wife of Siddhartha Gautama

Index